This book is dedicated to Aurora: I love you infinity.

Our Two Hearts
Copyright © 2023 by Annelisa Rheuben-Bathe

All rights reserved. No part of this publication may be reproduced, distributed, or transmitted in any form or by any means, including photocopying, recording, or other electronic or mechanical methods, without the prior written permission of the author, except in the case of brief quotations embodied in critical reviews and certain other non-commercial uses permitted by copyright law.

Tellwell Talent
www.tellwell.ca

ISBN
978-0-2288-9422-3 (Hardcover)
978-0-2288-9421-6 (Paperback)
978-0-2288-9685-2 (eBook)

Our Two Hearts

By Annelisa Rheuben-Bathe

The moment I saw you,
we would never be apart.
Right then and there, we were
bonded, heart to heart.

I instantly knew,
Life was forever changed.
As my heart made room
It was neatly arranged.

For right next to yours,
And there next to mine,
Our Two Hearts together
Forever interwined.

Whenever you feel
you might be alone,
Know I am with you
even after you're grown.

If ever we are past
your arm's length
Here's what to do
to give you strength:

Put your hands on
the left side of your chest.
Right there beside it,
put your fears to rest.

For no matter what,
and no matter where,
My heart, next to yours,
is always there.

Even if we yell,
don't speak,
or fight,
My love for you is endless,
no matter who's right.

I will always be with you,
wherever you go.
Hearts bonded together,
as I love you so.

Whether happy, excited,
angry or sad,
I will always love you,
in good times or bad.

Whenever you miss me,
or think I am gone,
Put your hands on our hearts
to carry on.

Remember this tool
and repeat it, please:
These two hands over
Our Two Hearts.
(You can do this with ease.)

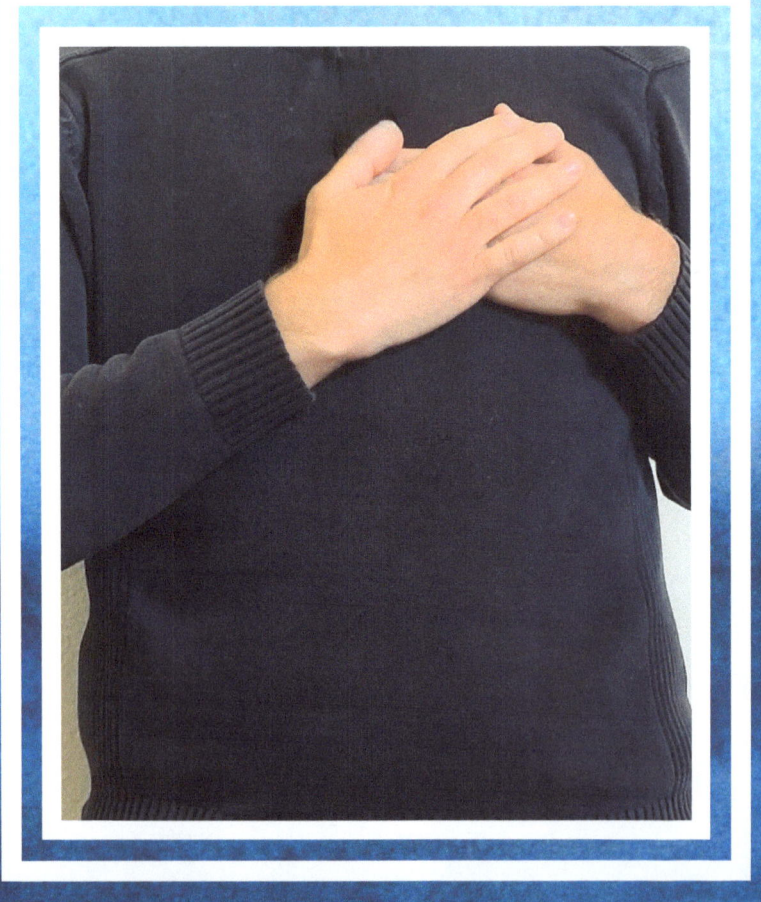

If you feel scared or lonely,
and you can't see me.
Know my heart is with you
And forever will be.

On any given day,
even if we're apart.
I will always be with you,
bonded heart to heart.

www.ingramcontent.com/pod-product-compliance
Lightning Source LLC
LaVergne TN
LVHW070047070526
838200LV00028B/417